# 27 ARTICLES

## T. E. LAWRENCE

### INTRODUCTION BY JOHN HULSMAN
### AFTERWORD BY DAVID RHODES

*Simon & Schuster*

NEW YORK LONDON TORONTO
SYDNEY NEW DELHI

Simon & Schuster
1230 Avenue of the Americas
New York, NY 10020

Introduction copyright 2017 by Dr. John C. Hulsman
Afterword copyright © 2017 by David Rhodes
*27 Articles* was originally published in 1917

First Simon & Schuster hardcover edition August 2017

SIMON & SCHUSTER and colophon are registered trademarks
of Simon & Schuster, Inc.

For information about special discounts for bulk purchases,
please contact Simon & Schuster Special Sales at 1-866-506-1949
or business@simonandschuster.com.

The Simon & Schuster Speakers Bureau can bring authors to
your live event. For more information or to book an event contact
the Simon & Schuster Speakers Bureau at 1-866-248-3049
or visit our website at www.simonspeakers.com.

Manufactured in the United States of America

1   3   5   7   9   10   8   6   4   2

Library of Congress Cataloging-in-Publication Data is available.

ISBN: 978-1-5011-8200-6
ISBN: 978-1-5011-8201-3 (ebook)

# Contents

# Contents

Introduction

# *Lawrence of Arabia, Forgotten Visionary*

John Hulsman

April 2017

Just before the start of the Iraq War, I was asked by the Council on Foreign Relations to serve on a task force aimed at advising the Bush administration on how to run Iraq after the fall of Saddam. It was soon after 9/11, and the neoconservative program of imposing democracy at the point of a gun was in full swing. Our mission was to devise a general blueprint for creating a stable country from scratch, or, as we skeptics put it at the time, how to add water and get George Washington.

This experience is what led me to bump

squarely into the work of Lawrence of Arabia. One of the points made incessantly by all the great and the good assembled for the Iraqi task force at the meeting was that, if nation building was to have a chance of success, inserting Western liberal democratic values into failed states like Iraq from outside sources was an absolute prerequisite. The discussion focused on just how fast we could make this happen, avoiding any mention of Iraq's unique history, politics, culture, ethnology, sociology, economic status, or religious orientation. What did these trifles matter compared with the Washington elite's view of how the world really ought to work?

Eventually, despite knowing that it would only cost me, I rose to my feet and said my piece. Though I mangled the exact quotation, I was close enough: "Do not try to do too much with your own hands. Better the Arabs do it tolerably than you do it perfectly. It is their war, and you are to help them, not to win it for them." To help them—not to dictate to them, manage them, bully them, ignore them, or lecture them—to help them help themselves. The quote was from T. E. Lawrence, though at the time I could not remember where I had read it.

I was heard out in stony silence, and after the meeting I was advised by my political allies that I had better get with the program. Instead, as Lawrence would have done, I went off into the desert, looking for a better way.

I sought out the quotation I had hazily recalled at the meeting and found it in T. E. Lawrence's *27 Articles*, written in August 1917, a primer for British officers serving in the Arab Revolt in World War I on how to work effectively with local peoples. As I read the articles and learned more about the man, it dawned on me that all the failed or partially failed attempts at nation building in the post–Cold War era—in Haiti, Somalia, Bosnia, Kosovo, Afghanistan, and Iraq—were intimately related. In every case they were based on the same analytically flawed worldview. Journeying into the intellectual desert, seeking out Lawrence of Arabia, turned out to be hugely rewarding.

For while conventional wisdom about nation building has proven depressingly (and predictably) wrong, there are answers out there: forgotten answers from another age, answers we are all in desperate need of rediscovering.

We must go back in time to the early twentieth century, exactly one hundred years ago, when an increasingly famous British subaltern was hastily scribbling some notes in the wastes of the Arabian Desert. For Lawrence was considering questions that go well beyond the particulars of fighting in World War I, or even how to do nation building: he's offering us nothing less than a wholly different worldview for how to work with others.

Despite being, next to his close friend Winston Churchill, the most famous Englishman of the twentieth century, T. E. Lawrence has remained an enigma. There have been more than thirty books on him, several plays, and one magnificent if inaccurate Oscar-winning movie, yet still Lawrence somehow evades us, as he wished to, remaining just out of reach.

Part of the problem is that in his short life

Lawrence was a true Renaissance man. He was an archaeologist, war photographer, mapmaker, intelligence officer, guerrilla fighter, political leader, diplomat, movie star, public policy intellectual, writer, linguist, thinker, and mechanic. His many talents seem designed to overwhelm us from getting a sense of what in him was central, and what was interesting but peripheral.

Misleadingly, Lawrence's incarnation as a war hero has tended to eclipse everything else. For most Americans, the basis of the Lawrence myth is the peerless David Lean film *Lawrence of Arabia*, which was released in 1962. Though playing fast and loose with the specific historical truth, Lean remained uncannily faithful to the spirit of Lawrence's epic account of the desert war, *Seven Pillars of Wisdom*. Peter O'Toole's portrayal of the desert hero is widely considered to be one of the best acting performances in screen history. The beloved movie took home the Academy Award for Best Picture (and six other Oscars) and regularly shows up on top ten lists of the best movies ever made. It is the image most of us retain of Lawrence.

Yet this iconic picture obscures far more than it reveals. Though viewed today primarily as a warrior prince, Lawrence was in reality far more important as a thinker. Through his direct personal experience, Lawrence happened upon a strategy for nation building in particular and leadership in general that was revolutionary then and remains so now—an intellectual philosophy forged in the cauldron of World War I. It might well have saved the world and the Middle East a great deal of subsequent historical agony if his views had carried the day.

In the *27 Articles*, written one hundred years ago as a practical guide for British officers serving with the Hashemite army in western Arabia and Syria, Lawrence quite brilliantly laid out a much wider philosophical basis for working with peoples on the cusp of nation building. While the articles—as is true of all historical documents—are a product of their time, containing an imperial ethos (and Lawrence was surely a fervent, if reformist, imperialist), more important, they put forward a forgotten philosophy that transcends the specific limits of their time and space. Lawrence ultimately respects the agency of local Arab stakeholders in a way that betters the vast majority of our modern efforts. This long-forgotten philosophy constitutes nothing less than an entirely workable blueprint for nation building in our own troubled era. Lawrence's policy primer had made the Arabs stakeholders in the outcome of their war, the primary actors in their own story of regeneration and renewal.

While the Arab Revolt against the Ottoman Empire was a "sideshow within a sideshow," in Lawrence's own view, unlike the carnage on the Western Front it yielded a decisive Allied victory. During the war in western Arabia and Greater Syria (today's Syria, Lebanon, Jordan, Israel, and Palestine), the charismatic Prince Faisal—Lawrence's comrade and close collaborator—possessed the rarest and most precious of attributes for nation building to succeed. In Arabia, Faisal was the unquestioned, rightful, legitimate representative of local political power. This local legitimacy was the cornerstone of Lawrence's very different philosophy and the policy methods that sprang from it. This simple, unimpeachable fact was the wellspring of Lawrence's entire revolutionary philosophy: one needs to start with the pieces already in play rather than imposing prefabricated ideals from afar.

Today, behind all the mythology surrounding the enigmatic Lawrence, the most important aspect of him, the man as thinker, lies waiting to be rediscovered. If his story helps provide the context for the greater tragedy of the Middle East for the rest of the twentieth century, his forgotten ideas laid out in the *27 Articles* provide an antidote to the tragedy's continuation.

In August 1917, the British High Command, belatedly realizing that they had no real idea how Lawrence had produced the miracle of capturing vital Aqaba with Faisal's ragtag Bedu army, tasked him with codifying what he had learned about the Arabs in a manual that could be used by other British officers serving in the field with the Hashemite troops.

It was feared that, given the good chance Lawrence might die, his unique knowledge of working with the Arab forces would be lost forever. So Lawrence, in the midst of the guerrilla campaign that followed Aqaba, somewhat grumpily began typing his *27 Articles* in the heat of the desert sun.

A brilliant mixture of political, military, and psychological analysis, *27 Articles* offers nothing less than a revolutionary new way for Western nation builders to look at the rest of the world. It was a century ahead of its time. Lawrence realized that in his particular case he could not win without the political support of the local Arab population in western Arabia and Greater Syria—but with their support, he could not lose.

First appearing in the *Arab Bulletin* on August 20, 1917, Lawrence stressed that the 27 general rules he propounded were based on his experiences in the Hejaz (western Arabia) and apply only to the Bedu. However, this is far too analytically modest. For with the *27 Articles* what Lawrence laid out was a startlingly original general philosophy for nation building writ large. More than this, Lawrence somewhat unwittingly tapped into a more general notion of what successful leadership actually amounts to.

# T. E. Lawrence

For Lawrence, local organic developments, specific cultural knowledge, and an emphasis on "the unique" are the keys to successful nation building. He stressed the conservative view of the eighteenth-century Anglo-Irish philosopher Edmund Burke that politics is an organic construction: like a plant it blossoms or perishes in the soil of a unique history, culture, and set of circumstances.

Lawrence's first general principle laid out in the *27 Articles* is, then, that local knowledge and particularism are the keys to nation-building success. Understanding and working with local culture and the politics that flow from it is what matters most. The second point in the *27 Articles* commands: "Learn all you can about your Ashraf and Bedu. Get to know their families, clans and tribes, friends and enemies, wells, hills and roads."

This is because—as America has found recently to its own bitter cost—it is impossible to transform a society about which one knows almost nothing. Lawrence's diametrically opposed admonition suggests that learning about the peoples one is attempting to help is far more important than forcing them to accept Western norms that have played no historical role in their culture.

In Lawrence's case, because he underlined the need to work entirely within the existing Bedu social and political structure, his initiatives had a real chance of taking root and acquiring the local support that makes policy longevity possible. Working *with* the grain of history contrasts with the usual tired Western approach of grafting foreign ideas onto a native culture, which is often rejected in short order. On the other hand, Lawrence's approach makes local buy-in, which is absolutely vital for successful nation building, at least a possibility.

Lawrence tells an amusing story about himself, illustrating what happens when a Westerner takes charge of another people's destiny: he quickly gets out of his depth. During an atypical guerrilla raid, he was forced to lead an expedition personally, rather than serve in his usual role of advisor to the local tribal chieftain.

Lawrence later ruefully remembered the debacle. "I had to be OC [officer in charge] of the whole expedition. This is not a job which should be undertaken by foreigners, since we have not so intimate a knowledge of Arab families . . . I had to adjudicate in twelve cases of assault with weapons, four camel-thefts, one marriage-settlement, fourteen feuds, two evil eyes, and a bewitchment. These affairs take up all one's spare time." While Lawrence typically sees the humor in the situation there is real peril at work here. A lack of deep knowledge required to adequately adjudicate these disputes risked desta-bilizing the whole expedition, as it would invariably lead to chaos and infighting. How much more is this the case when, unlike Lawrence, local knowledge is almost entirely lacking, as occurred in both Ameri-can misadventures in Vietnam and Iraq.

It is a measure of Lawrence's success in mas-tering a true understanding of Bedu culture that it was Faisal himself who first suggested he wear the robes of a tribal chieftain, which illustrated as noth-ing else could that the Arab tribesmen considered Lawrence "one of us."

In fact, Faisal came to be vexed on the rare subsequent occasions when Lawrence appeared in regulation British khaki, as if this meant he was breaking faith with the honorary tribal membership the Arabs had bestowed on him. Lawrence makes clear in Article 18 of the *27 Articles* that "if you can wear Arab kit when with the tribes, you will acquire their mutual trust and intimacy to a degree impossible in uniform."

Wearing Arab dress became the iconic symbol of Lawrence's cultural understanding of and affinity for the Arab world, a metaphorical badge of honor, underlining his radically different approach of working with the Bedu in a bottom-up fashion. The final point of the *27 Articles* makes this crystal clear: "The beginning and ending of the secret of handling Arabs is an unremitting study of them." This is true for every single culture in the world.

The second general principle underlying the *27 Articles* is the absolute primacy of politics. Lawrence understood that local Arab politics superseded whatever was happening on the battlefield against the Ottoman Empire. In fact, things worked the other way around: the military outcome of the Arab Revolt was dependent on the political disposition of the locals. The key to victory was simple:

gain local civilian sympathy. For the campaign to succeed, "It must have a friendly population, not actively friendly, but sympathetic to the point of not betraying rebel movements to the enemy. Rebellions can be made by 2 percent active in a striking force, and 98 percent passively sympathetic."

Crucially, Lawrence never forgot that for Faisal and the Arabs the ultimate goal of the war was political: to forge an Arab nation. For nation building to be successful, determining the organic local unit of politics is key. In the case of the Bedu it was the fiercely independent tribe and not the Western preference for some sort of Jeffersonian construct. Lawrence squared this circle by working with Arab political realities, not ignoring them. The unit of politics in the Bedu world was tribal and local, whether he liked it or not. As he made clear, "The largest indigenous political entity in settled Syria is only the village under its sheikh, and in patriarchal Syria under its chief."

Lawrence understood that such a fractured political reality called for a "minimum of central power," as confederation organically meshed with the dominant localism that defined Arab politics in Faisal's army as well as in Greater Syria. Lawrence, knowing his comrades culturally, could see that less government for them was better, as it suited their lifestyle as well as their intrinsic political worldview.

Tailoring a political system to fit the local unit of politics, rather than imposing a one-size-fits-all overly centralized government on others, is a major insight Lawrence has to teach the failed nation builders of today. To make nation building work, first one needs to find out how the people you are dealing with organize themselves to get things done, and then to operate within this already existing, organic system.

The third key theme of the *27 Articles* is that Lawrence was acutely aware that as an outsider he had to be above local politics; he could not be seen to be in the business of picking political winners and losers. As the primary British representative in Faisal's army, he knew that his personal favor or disfavor of particular Arab leaders would be used by local elites to discredit those he sided with.

They would quickly be accused of being stooges, lackeys of the British government, which would cost them the very local legitimacy that made them worth working with in the first place. Ironically, by making his support transparent, Lawrence would be doing a disservice to the leaders he did value, undermining their effectiveness with their people.

As Article 8 makes clear, "Avoid being identified too long or too often with any tribal sheikh, even if C.O. [Commanding Officer] of the expedition . . . Sherifs are above all blood-feuds and local rivalries, and form the only principle of unity among the Arabs. Let your name be therefore coupled always with a Sherif's, and share his attitude towards the tribes." This imaginative approach allowed Lawrence to expertly navigate the treacherous shoals of inter-Bedu politics.

Perhaps most important, Lawrence believed that nation building would not succeed unless it was advanced by the locals themselves. In his masterpiece, *Seven Pillars of Wisdom,* he makes clear that the Arab Revolt "was an Arab war waged and led by Arabs for an Arab aim in Arabia." Through the trial by fire of the Great War, the Arabs under Faisal had largely liberated themselves.

For moral reasons, but also for very practical ones, the local people must be the primary stake-holders in nation-building efforts. Above all, the West should help but not dictate, facilitate but not domi-nate, influence but not lead, advise but not manage. The differences in these terms are not semantic. For they denote wholly different approaches to nation building. Lawrence recognized that there are real limits to what Westerners can do working with local cultures and, as such, limits to what should be un-dertaken. In Lawrence's particular historical case, the only way the Arab Revolt worked was when Western and Bedu interests aligned over expelling the Ottomans from Arabia. Far too often, too much is attempted by outside Western powers, as "regime change" without working with local interests is al-most never going to work.

Fourth and finally, Lawrence understood that local political stability was key to peace in the Middle East. Faisal, as leader of the Bedu, was the personification of this political truth. Though short, soft-spoken, and shy, even as a young man the shrewd Faisal was a force to be reckoned with. As the son of Emir Hussein, the keeper of the Muslim holy places of Mecca and Medina and directly descended from the Prophet Muhammad, Faisal enjoyed the unquestioned religious legitimacy this conveyed upon his Hashemite family.

In addition, Faisal was uniquely acceptable to the loosely aligned tribes of the Arabian Desert and Greater Syria: the Ruwalla, the Serahin, the Bani Sakhr, and the Howeitat. As the Great War progressed and the Hashemite cause picked up steam, not only had Faisal given them victory (not a small consideration in Arab culture), he also spoke their dialect of Arabic, understood their tribal structure, and knew their histories. In short, Faisal had the golden advantage of political legitimacy based on shared cultural ties with his men.

Lawrence, from their first fateful meeting in Hamra in Arabia in 1916, had recognized that Faisal alone possessed this magic elixir. He saw his own role as advisory. As he stressed in Article 3 of the *27 Articles*, "Never give orders to anyone at all. . . . Your place is advisory, and your advice is due to the commander alone. Let him see this is your conception of your duty, and that his is to be the sole executive of your joint plans."

Article 11 continues in this vein: "Wave a Sherif in front of you like a banner and hide your own mind and person." During the Arab Revolt, all major military operations Lawrence participated in were led by an Arab commander in chief, with Lawrence in a vital but supporting role as advisor. In Article 14, Lawrence underlines that, paradoxically, this restrained, secondary role for himself is the key to exercising power: "While very difficult to drive, the Bedu are easy to lead, if [you] have the patience to bear with them. The less apparent your interferences the more your influence."

Lawrence's philosophy was not the product of some sort of Western Orientalist plot; it was not a sophisticated way of fooling the Arabs into a more nuanced form of submission. Rather it amounts to a far more thoughtful and effective way for Westerners to work with developing nations, a way of thinking that has the potential to serve the interests of both. In the case of the Great War, both the Hashemites and the British wanted to expel the Ottomans from their far-away Arabian possessions. This basic strategic commonality was a start. Coupled with Lawrence's unique insight to let the Arabs take the lead in their own story of national liberation, it amounted to a strikingly successful policy.

As at Carchemish, where a young prewar Lawrence supervised an archaeological dig on the Turkish-Syrian border, Lawrence's overall goal in the Arab Revolt was to enable the Hashemite army to do its own work better. As he wrote to his confidante and adopted mother figure Charlotte Shaw, the wife of playwright George Bernard Shaw, after the war, "All of my experience of the Arabs was of the God-father role. My object . . . was always to make them stand on their own feet." In the common shared interests of both the British and the Hashemites, Lawrence wanted to help the Arabs help themselves.

Lawrence's very different nation-building phi-

losophy was tested in the most unforgiving class-
room imaginable—the real world engulfed in the
horrors of global war. Lawrence's friend and biog-
rapher Robert Graves estimated that the British
government spent around ten million pounds on
the Arab Revolt, and endured a paltry score or
so of British casualties in fighting the Ottomans
alongside Prince Faisal. Given the fantastic results,
it was Lawrence's brilliant, if unorthodox, philosophy that made this British expenditure a bargain
at this price.

For all his undoubted brilliance as a soldier
and a man of dash, it is T. E. Lawrence's role as a
thinker ahead of his time that is most valuable for
the world we live in. Lawrence's forgotten nation-
building philosophy—with an intellectual and policy reach well beyond the immediate specifics and
place of the Arab Revolt and the time of the Great
War—points to a very different strategy of leadership and nation building from the top-down failures we see today. While Lawrence has long been
dead, the days ahead cry out for a resurrection of
his thought.

# 27 Articles

T. E. Lawrence

August 20, 1917

The following notes have been expressed in commandment form for greater clarity and to save words. They are, however, only my personal conclusions, arrived at gradually while I worked in the Hejaz and now put on paper as stalking horses for beginners in the Arab armies. They are meant to apply only to Bedu; townspeople or Syrians require totally different treatment. They are of course not suitable to any other person's need, or applicable unchanged in any particular situation. Handling Hejaz Arabs is an art, not a science, with exceptions and no obvious rules. At the same time we have a great chance there; the Sherif trusts us, and has given us the position (towards his Government) which the Germans wanted to win in Turkey. If we are tactful, we can at once retain his goodwill and carry out our job, but to succeed we have got to put into it all the interest and skill we possess.

## *Article 1.*

Go easy for the first few weeks. A bad start is difficult to atone for, and the Arabs form their judgments on externals that we ignore. When you have reached the inner circle in a tribe, you can do as you please with yourself and them.

# T. E. Lawrence

## *Article 2.*

Learn all you can about your Ashraf and Bedu. Get to know their families, clans and tribes, friends and enemies, wells, hills and roads. Do all this by listening and by indirect inquiry. Do not ask questions. Get to speak their dialect of Arabic, not yours. Until you can understand their allusions, avoid getting deep into conversation or you will drop bricks. Be a little stiff at first.

*Article 3.*

In matters of business deal only with the commander of the army, column, or party in which you serve. Never give orders to anyone at all, and reserve your directions or advice for the C.O., however great the temptation (for efficiency's sake) of dealing with his underlings. Your place is advisory, and your advice is due to the commander alone. Let him see that this is your conception of your duty, and that his is to be the sole executive of your joint plans.

### *Article 4.*

Win and keep the confidence of your leader. Strengthen his prestige at your expense before others when you can. Never refuse or quash schemes he may put forward; but ensure that they are put forward in the first instance privately to you. Always approve them, and after praise modify them insensibly, causing the suggestions to come from him, until they are in accord with your own opinion. When you attain this point, hold him to it, keep a tight grip of his ideas, and push them forward as firmly as possibly, but secretly, so that to one but himself (and he not too clearly) is aware of your pressure.

*Article 5.*

Remain in touch with your leader as constantly and unobtrusively as you can. Live with him, that at meal times and at audiences you may be naturally with him in his tent. Formal visits to give advice are not so good as the constant dropping of ideas in casual talk. When stranger sheikhs come in for the first time to swear allegiance and offer service, clear out of the tent. If their first impression is of foreigners in the confidence of the Sherif, it will do the Arab cause much harm.

*Article 6.*

Be shy of too close relations with the
subordinates of the expedition. Contin-
ual intercourse with them will make it
impossible for you to avoid going behind
or beyond the instructions that the Arab
C.O. has given them on your advice, and
in so disclosing the weakness of his position you altogether destroy your own.

*Article 7.*

Treat the sub-chiefs of your force quite easily and lightly. In this way you hold yourself above their level. Treat the leader, if a Sherif, with respect. He will return your manner and you and he will then be alike, and above the rest. Precedence is a serious matter among the Arabs, and you must attain it.

*Article 8.*

Your ideal position is when you are present and not noticed. Do not be too intimate, too prominent, or too earnest. Avoid being identified too long or too often with any tribal sheikh, even if C.O. of the expedition. To do your work you must be above jealousies, and you lose prestige if you are associated with a tribe or clan, and its inevitable feuds. Sherifs are above all blood-feuds and local rivalries, and form the only principle of unity among the Arabs. Let your name therefore be coupled always with a Sherif's, and share his attitude towards the tribes. When the moment comes for action put yourself publicly under his orders. The Bedu will then follow suit.

*Article 9.*

Magnify and develop the growing conception of the Sherifs as the natural aristocracy of the Arabs. Intertribal jealousies make it impossible for any sheikh to attain a commanding position, and the only hope of union in nomad Arabs is that the Ashraf be universally acknowledged as the ruling class. Sherifs are half-townsmen, half-nomad, in manner and life, and have the instinct of command. Mere merit and money would be insufficient to obtain such recognition; but the Arab reverence for pedigree and the Prophet gives hope for the ultimate success of the Ashraf.

# T. E. Lawrence

*Article 10.*

Call your Sherif "Sidi" in public and in private. Call other people by their ordinary names, without title. In intimate conversation call a Sheikh "Abu Annad," "Akhu Alia" or some similar by-name.

### *Article 11.*

The foreigner and Christian is not a popular person in Arabia. However friendly and informal the treatment of yourself may be, remember always that your foundations are very sandy ones. Wave a Sherif in front of you like a banner and hide your own mind and person. If you succeed, you will have hundreds of miles of country and thousands of men under your orders, and for this it is worth bartering the outward show.

*Article 12.*

Cling tight to your sense of humour. You will need it every day. A dry irony is the most useful type, and repartee of a personal and not too broad character will double your influence with the chiefs. Reproof, if wrapped up in some smiling form, will carry further and last longer than the most violent speech. The power of mimicry or parody is valuable, but use it sparingly, for wit is more dignified than humour. Do not cause a laugh at a Sherif except among Sherifs.

## *Article 13.*

Never lay hands on an Arab; you degrade yourself. You may think the resultant obvious increase of outward respect a gain to you, but what you have really done is to build a wall between you and their inner selves. It is difficult to keep quiet when everything is being done wrong, but the less you lose your temper the greater your advantage. Also then you will not go mad yourself.

# T. E. Lawrence

*Article 14.*

While very difficult to drive, the Bedu are easy to lead, if: have the patience to bear with them. The less apparent your interferences the more your influence. They are willing to follow your advice and do what you wish, but they do not mean you or anyone else to be aware of that. It is only after the end of all annoyances that you find at bottom their real fund of goodwill.

*Article 15.*

Do not try to do too much with your own hands. Better the Arabs do it tolerably than that you do it perfectly. It is their war, and you are to help them, not to win it for them. Actually, also, under the very odd conditions of Arabia, your practical work will not be as good as, perhaps, you think it is.

*Article 16.*

If you can, without being too lavish, fore-stall presents to yourself. A well-placed gift is often most effective in winning over a suspicious sheikh. Never receive a present without giving a liberal return, but you may delay this return (while letting its ultimate certainty be known) if you require a particular service from the giver. Do not let them ask you for things, since their greed will then make them look upon you only as a cow to milk.

*Article 17.*

Wear an Arab headcloth when with a tribe. Bedu have a malignant prejudice against the hat, and believe that our persistence in wearing it (due probably to British obstinacy of dictation) is founded on some immoral or irreligious principle. A thick headcloth forms a good protection against the sun, and if you wear a hat your best Arab friends will be ashamed of you in public.

# T. E. Lawrence

## Article 18.

Disguise is not advisable. Except in special areas, let it be clearly known that you are a British officer and a Christian. At the same time, if you can wear Arab kit when with the tribes, you will acquire their trust and intimacy to a degree impossible in uniform. It is, however, dangerous and difficult. They make no special allowances for you when you dress like them. Breaches of etiquette not charged against a foreigner are not condoned to you in Arab clothes. You will be like an actor in a foreign theatre, playing a part day and night for months, without rest, and for an anxious stake. Complete success, which is when the Arabs forget your strangeness and speak naturally before you, counting you as one of themselves, is perhaps only attainable in character: while half-success (all that most of us will strive for; the other costs too much) is easier to win in British things, and you yourself will last longer, physically and mentally, in the comfort that they mean. Also then the Turks will not hang you, when you are caught.

*Article 19.*

If you wear Arab things, wear the best. Clothes are significant among the tribes, and you must wear the appropriate, and appear at ease in them. Dress like a Sherif, if they agree to it.

*Article 20.*

If you wear Arab things at all, go the whole
way. Leave your English friends and customs
on the coast, and fall back on Arab habits entirely. It is possible, starting thus level with
them, for the European to beat the Arabs at
their own game, for we have stronger motives
for our action, and put more heart into it than
they. If you can surpass them, you have taken
an immense stride toward complete success,
but the strain of living and thinking in a foreign and half-understood language, the savage
food, strange clothes, and stranger ways, with
the complete loss of privacy and quiet, and
the impossibility of ever relaxing your watch-
ful imitation of the others for months on end,
provide such an added stress to the ordinary
difficulties of dealing with the Bedu, the cli-
mate, and the Turks, that this road should not
be chosen without serious thought.

*Article 21.*

Religious discussions will be frequent. Say what you like about your own side, and avoid criticism of theirs, unless you know that the point is external, when you may score heavily by proving it so. With the Bedu, Islam is so all-pervading an element that there is little religiosity, little fervour, and no regard for externals. Do not think from their conduct that they are careless. Their conviction of the truth of their faith, and its share in every act and thought and principle of their daily life is so intimate and intense as to be unconscious, unless roused by opposition. Their religion is as much a part of nature to them as is sleep or food.

*Article 22.*

Do not try to trade on what you know of fighting. The Hejaz confounds ordinary tactics. Learn the Bedu principles of war as thoroughly and as quickly as you can, for till you know them your advice will be no good to the Sherif. Unnumbered generations of tribal raids have taught them more about some parts of the business than we will ever know. In familiar conditions they fight well, but strange events cause panic. Keep your unit small. Their raiding parties are usually from one hundred to two hundred men, and if you take a crowd they only get confused. Also their sheikhs, while admirable company commanders, are too "set" to learn to handle the equivalents of battalions or regiments. Don't attempt unusual things, unless they appeal to the sporting instinct Bedu have so strongly, unless success is obvious. If the objective is a good one (booty) they will attack like fiends, they are splendid scouts, their mobility gives you the advantage that will win this local war, they make proper use of their knowledge of the country (don't take tribesmen to places they do not know), and the gazelle-hunters, who form a proportion of the better men, are great shots at visible targets. A sheikh from one tribe cannot give orders to men from another; a Sherif is necessary to command a mixed tribal force. If there is plunder in prospect, and the odds are at all equal, you will win. Do not waste Bedu attacking trenches (they will not stand casualties) or in trying to defend a position, for they cannot sit still without slacking. The more unorthodox and Arab your proceedings, the more likely you are to have the Turks cold, for they lack initiative and expect you to. Don't play for safety.

T. E. Lawrence

*Article 23.*

The open reason that Bedu give you for action or inaction may be true, but always there will be better reasons left for you to divine. You must find these inner reasons (they will be denied, but are none the less in operation) before shaping your arguments for one course or other. Allusion is more effective than logical exposition: they dislike concise expression. Their minds work just as ours do, but on different premises. There is nothing unreasonable, incomprehensible, or inscrutable in the Arab. Experience of them, and knowledge of their prejudices will enable you to foresee their attitude and possible course of action in nearly every case.

## Article 24.

Do not mix Bedu and Syrians, or trained men and tribesmen. You will get work out of neither, for they hate each other. I have never seen a successful combined operation, but many failures. In particular, ex-officers of the Turkish army, however Arab in feelings and blood and language, are hopeless with Bedu. They are narrow minded in tactics, unable to adjust themselves to irregular warfare, clumsy in Arab etiquette, swollen-headed to the extent of being incapable of politeness to a tribesman for more than a few minutes, impatient, and, usually, helpless without their troops on the road and in action. Your orders (if you were unwise enough to give any) would be more readily obeyed by Beduins than those of any Mohammedan Syrian officer. Arab townsmen and Arab tribesmen regard each other mutually as poor relations, and poor relations are much more objectionable than poor strangers.

## *Article 25.*

In spite of ordinary Arab example, avoid too free talk about women. It is as difficult a subject as religion, and their standards are so unlike our own that a remark, harmless in English, may appear as unrestrained to them, as some of their statements would look to us, if translated literally.

## Article 26.

Be as careful of your servants as of yourself. If you want a sophisticated one you will probably have to take an Egyptian, or a Sudani, and unless you are very lucky he will undo on trek much of the good you so laboriously effect. Arabs will cook rice and make coffee for you, and leave you if required to do unmanly work like cleaning boots or washing. They are only really possible if you are in Arab kit. A slave brought up in the Hejaz is the best servant, but there are rules against British subjects owning them, so they have to be lent to you. In any case, take with you an Ageyli or two when you go up country. They are the most efficient couriers in Arabia, and understand camels.

# T. E. Lawrence

*Article 27.*

The beginning and ending of the secret of handling Arabs is unremitting study of them. Keep always on your guard; never say an unnecessary thing: watch yourself and your companions all the time: hear all that passes, search out what is going on beneath the surface, read their characters, discover their tastes and their weaknesses and keep everything you find out to yourself. Bury yourself in Arab circles, have no interests and no ideas except the work in hand, so that your brain is saturated with one thing only, and you realize your part deeply enough to avoid the little slips that would counteract the painful work of weeks. Your success will be proportioned to the amount of mental effort you devote to it.

# Afterword

## David Rhodes

### April 2017

"Do not try to do too much with your own hands."

That's how Article 15 begins. Eloquently, it makes an argument that has helped define Western views of the Mideast since 1917. But it might as well tell you how to manage a competitive business in 2017. Never mind that Lawrence himself said the *27 Articles* "are meant to apply only to Bedu."

Because the articles are about insurgency, counterinsurgency, . . . and manipulation. Basically, they are about what's going on outside your window and in the ether of the present day.

A generation ago there was a fad on Wall Street for Sun Tzu. Traders in the 1980s quoted from the

Chinese strategist's *Art of War*. So what's the difference?

If Lawrence is about shaping events by manipulation, Sun is famously about shaping events by deception. And maybe deception helped sell stock, when people could still remember holding paper certificates. Now it sounds like Dire Straits singing about microwave ovens and color TVs in "Money for Nothing": dated.

No ancient martial philosophy is likely to feel current in today's workplaces. Nor should it. Lawrence was flawed, in ways historians continue to debate. Blowing up a railway, hastening the demise of the Ottomans, securing an Islamist theocracy, advancing British imperialism, and inspiring an epic motion picture are not all positive outcomes for the world (although the movie is pretty good).

But Lawrence's theories, arrived at in the privation of the Arabian Desert one hundred years ago, actually make sense when applied to today's global, asymmetric, information-overloaded challenges. We don't mass armies anymore—on physical battlefields or in the server farms that arguably replaced them. It's hard to know where the threats are coming from, or how to confront them.

And so let Lawrence be your guide to the present situation. "Go easy for the first few weeks. A bad start is difficult to atone for"—true. Always "learn all you can" through "unremitting study." "Your foundations are very sandy ones" is a good check on corporate and management arrogance. "Do not try to trade on what you know of fighting"—because who likes a gossip? "Cling tight to your sense of humor"—for sanity.

When you read "religious discussions will be frequent" substitute "political" for "religious" and consider the perils of the modern workplace for many people. It's hard to avoid giving (or taking) offense.

And then maybe the greatest of all for its application to the present day: Article 8. "Your ideal position is when you are present and not noticed." Lawrence meant that "to do your work you must be above jealousies" and keep the initiative. Don't give in to ego and become distracted from achieving the objective.

# T. E. Lawrence

A colleague in journalism suggested to me that what Lawrence did have in common with the best reporters (and did not have in common with the worst excesses of his age) was he was there. Present. On the ground, developing an understanding of people and places.

The *27 Articles* are a cultural study and appreciation. In a way they're also a motivational speech, recognizing potential in any situation. What do we really know "of fighting" or anything else? Nothing can be accomplished without an understanding of the people who are setting out to accomplish it. Whether they are people like us or people unlike us.

# About the Authors

T. E. Lawrence, popularly known as Lawrence of Arabia, lived from 1888 to 1935. He was a British military officer and diplomat, acting as a crucial liaison with Arab forces during the Arab Revolt against the Ottoman Empire from 1916 to 1918. His life is the basis for the 1962 film *Lawrence of Arabia*, and his best-known book is *Seven Pillars of Wisdom*, describing Lawrence's experiences during the revolt, while *27 Articles* summarizes his techniques and tactics.

John Hulsman is a foreign policy expert and life member of the Council on Foreign Relations. He is president and cofounder of John C. Hulsman Enterprises, a global political risk consulting firm. He has a PhD in International Relations from the University of St. Andrews in Scotland, and is the author of several books, including a biography of Lawrence of Arabia titled *To Begin the World Over Again*.

David Rhodes is president of CBS News, where he oversees the award-winning news division's programming on broadcast, radio and digital platforms, including CBSN, the first 24/7 anchored streaming news network. He became a Young Global Leader of the World Economic Forum in 2013 and is a member of the International Media Council at the annual meetings in Davos. He graduated from Rice University and currently sits on the board of trustees and the James A Baker III Institute Advisory Board. He lives with his wife, Emma, and two children in New York City.